MW00901981

TABLE OF CONTENTS

The Origin and Historical Foundation of Deliverance in the Bible.

Job 38:6 Whereupon are the foundations thereof fastened? Or who laid the corner stone thereof;

Job 38:7 When the morning stars sang together, and all the sons of God shouted for joy?

Luke 10:17 And the seventy returned again with joy, saying, Lord, even the devils are subject unto us through thy name.

Luke 10:18 And he said unto them; I beheld Satan as lightning fall from heaven.

Here we see the law of double reference in scripture when Jesus both speaks of Satan's fall in the past before Adam and Eve were created and the what he saw in the spirit when the disciples went preaching the Gospel in every city and him being there when Satan and 1/3 of the angel rebelled against God.

LAW OF DOUBLE REFERENCE Defined: The Law of Double Reference is the principle of associating similar or related ideas that, are usually separated from one another by long periods of time. Which are blended with a single thought or idea?

Rev 12:4 And his tail drew the third part of the stars of heaven, and did cast them to the earth: and the dragon stood before the woman which was ready to be delivered, for to devour her child as soon as it was born.

THE THIRD PART OF STARS: Are considered angels that fell with Satan during the rebelion called "Sons of God in Job 38:6).

Sons of God (Heb: bənê hā'ĕlōhîm, בנ האלהים) is a phrase used in the Hebrew Bible. Bene elohim are part of different Jewish angelic hierarchies.

Rev 12:7 And there was war in heaven: Michael and his angels fought against the dragon; and the dragon fought and his angels,

Rev 12:8 And prevailed not; neither was their place found any more in heaven.

Rev 12:9 And the great dragon was cast out, that old serpent, called the Devil, and Satan, which deceived the whole world: he was cast out into the earth, and his angels were cast out with him.

Luke 10:1 After these things the Lord appointed other seventy also, and sent them two and two before his face into every city and place, whither he himself would come. KJV

In Like 10:1 we see the warfare Jesus saw as he sent the disciples out tow and by two in every city, which was much like the warfare he saw in heaven during the fall of Satan and the 1/3 of his angels.

Translating the word **"City"** in this verse you will see the true nature of the warfare in the spirit Jesus was talking about.

CITY Defined: NT:4172 polis (pol'-is); probably from the same as NT:4171, or perhaps from NT:4183; a town (properly, with walls, of greater or less size): KJV - city.

CITY Defined: NT:4171 polemos (pol'-em-os); from pelomai (to bustle); warfare (literally or figuratively; a single encounter or a series): KJV - battle, fight, war.

(Biblesoft's New Exhaustive Strong's Numbers and Concordance with Expanded Greek-Hebrew Dictionary. Copyright © 1994, 2003, 2006 Biblesoft, Inc. and International Bible Translators, Inc.)

After the rebellion and fall of Satan and 1/3 of the angels which were manifested in many ranks, forms and positions throughout the universe.

RANK OF ANGELS

To understand the casting down of Satan and angels that followed him, one must see how they rule areas of creation during and after the rebellion. Not a single group rebelled but a mixture of them formally served God the father but now joined Satan.

The list I will give you below is to help you see rank and imagine the losing some of the brethren who use to do the same job but now some on Satan's side.

Paul's Description of Their Hierarchy

Eph 6:1212 For we wrestle not against flesh and blood, but against principalities, against powers, against the rulers of the darkness of this world, against spiritual wickedness in high places. KJV

Jessie Penn-Lewis defines the satanic forces described in Ephesians 6:12

For the Satanic forces described in Eph. 6: 12, are shown to be divided into

(1) "Principalities"--force and dominion dealing with nations and governments;

(2) "Powers"-- having authority and power of action in all the spheres open to them;

(3) " World- rulers"--governing the darkness, and blindness of the world at large;

(4) "Wicked spirits" in the heavenly places--their forces being directed in, and upon the Church of Jesus Christ, in "wiles," "fiery darts," onslaughts, and every conceivable deception over "doctrines" which they are capable of planning.

Penn-Lewis, Jessie (2010-11-13). War on the Saints (Original, Unabridged 1912 Edition) (Kindle Locations 286-292). . Kindle Edition.

The First Sphere

Seraphim - singular "Seraph"), mentioned in Isaiah 6:1-7 are the highest angelic class and serve as the caretakers of God's throne and continuously shout praises: "Holy, holy, holy is the Lord of hosts; the whole earth is full of his glory!"

Isa 6:2 Above it stood the seraphims: each one had six wings; with twain he covered his face, and with twain he covered his feet, and with twain he did fly.

Isa 6:3 And one cried unto another, and said, Holy, holy, holy, is the Lord of hosts: the whole earth is full of his glory. KJV

Cherubim - Cherubim have four faces: one of each a man, an ox, a lion, and an eagle. They have four conjoined wings covered with eyes, a lion's body figure, and they have ox's feet. Cherubim guard the way to the tree of life in the Garden of Eden (Genesis 3:24)[3] and the throne of God (Ezekiel 28:14-16)

Gen 3:24 So he drove out the man; and he placed at the east of the garden of Eden Cherubims, and a flaming sword which turned every way, to keep the way of the tree of life. KJV

Thrones or Ophanim - The "Thrones" (Greek: thronoi, pl. of thronos) or Elders, also known as the Erelim or Ophanim, are a class of celestial beings mentioned by Paul of Tarsus in Colossians 1:16 (New Testament). They are living symbols of God's justice and authority, and have as one of their symbols the throne.

Col 1:16 16 For by him were all things created, that are in heaven, and that are in earth, visible and invisible, whether they be thrones, or dominions, or principalities, or powers: all things were created by him, and for him: KJV

The Second Sphere

The "Dominions" (lat. dominatio, plural dominationes, also translated from the Greek term kyriotetes, of kyriotes, as "Lordships") or "Dominations" are presented as the hierarchy of celestial beings "Lordships"

The Dominions, regulate the duties of lower angels. It is only with extreme rarity that the angelic lords make themselves physically known to humans. They are also the angels who preside over nations.

The Dominions are believed to look like divinely beautiful humans with a pair of feathered wings, much like the common representation of angels, but they may be distinguished from other groups by wielding orbs of light fastened to the heads of their scepters or on the pommel (front) of their swords.

Virtues - The "Virtues" or "Strongholds" lay beyond the ophanim (Thrones/Wheels). Their primary duty is to supervise the movements of the heavenly bodies in order to ensure that the cosmos remains in order.

The term appears to be linked to the attribute "might", from the Greek root dynamis (pl. dynameis) in Ephesians 1:21, which is also translated as "Virtue".

Eph 1:21 Far above all principality, and power, and might, and dominion, and every name that is named, not only in this world, but also in that which is to come:

Powers or Authorities (lat. potestas (f), pl. potestates), or "Authorities", from the Greek exousiai, pl. of exousia (see Greek root in Eph 3:10), appear to collaborate, in power and authority, with the Principalities (Rulers).

The Powers are the bearers of conscience and the keepers of history. They are also the warrior angels created to be completely loyal to God.

Some believe that no Power has ever fallen from grace, but another theory states that Satan was the Chief of the Powers before he Fell (see also Ephesians 6:12). Their duty is to oversee the distribution of power among humankind, hence their name

The Principalities - are shown wearing a crown and carrying a sceptre. Their duty also is said to be to carry out the orders given to them by the Dominions and bequeath blessings to the material world. Their task is to oversee groups of people. They are the educators and guardians of the realm of earth. Like beings related to the world of the germinal ideas, they are said to inspire living things to many things such as art or science

Archangel - The word "archangel" comes from the Greek ἀρχάγγελος (archangĕlŏs), meaning chief angel, a translation of the Hebrew רב־מלאך (rav-mal'ákh) [11] It derives from the Greek archō, meaning to be first in rank or power; and angĕlŏs which means messenger or envoy. The word is only used twice in the New Testament: 1 Thessalonians 4:16 and Jude 1:9. Only Archangels Gabriel and Michael are mentioned by name in the New Testament

Jude 9 Yet Michael the archangel, when contending with the devil he disputed about the body of Moses, durst not bring against him a railing accusation, but said, The Lord rebuke thee KJV

Luke 1:26 6 And in the sixth month the angel Gabriel was sent from God unto a city of Galilee, named Nazareth, KJV

The name of the archangel Raphael appears only in the Book of Tobit (Tobias). Tobit is considered Deuterocanonical by Roman Catholics (both Eastern and Western Rites) and Eastern Orthodox Christians.

• Another possible interpretation of the seven archangels is that these seven are the seven spirits of God that stand before the throne described in the Book of Enoch, and in the Book of Revelation.[12]

Rev 3:1 And unto the angel of the church in Sardis write; These things saith he that hath the seven Spirits of God, and the seven stars; I know thy works, that thou hast a name that thou livest, and art dead. KJV

The Book of Tobit is also read by Anglicans and Lutherans, but not by Reformed Christians or Baptists. Raphael said to Tobias that he was "one of the seven who stand before the Lord", and it is generally believed that Michael and Gabriel are two of the other six.

• **The Seven Archangels** are said to be the guardian angels of nations and countries, and are concerned with the issues and events surrounding these, including politics, military matters, commerce and trade: e.g.

• **Archangel Michael** is traditionally seen as the protector of Israel and of the ecclesia (Gr. root ekklesia from the New Testament passages), theologically equated as the Church, the forerunner of the spiritual New Israel.

Isa 11:1-2 – THE SEVEN SPIRITS OF GOD ALL ARE ONE SPIRIT

Deut 6:4 Hear, O Israel: The Lord our God is one Lord:

The "Sevenfold Ministry of the Spirit" interpretation holds that the seven Spirits refer to <u>Book of Isaiah </u>11:2. In this interpretation, "The "seven Spirits" represent the sevenfold ministry of the Spirit as depicted in Isaiah 11:2

Sevenfold may also be connected with the Biblical understanding of the number 7 representing perfection. The "Seven Fold Spirit of God" could be the "perfect" Spirit of God, the Holy Spirit

Isa 11:2 And the spirit of the Lord shall rest upon him, the spirit of wisdom and understanding, the spirit of counsel and might, the spirit of knowledge and of the fear of the Lord; KJV

Isa 11:1 And there shall come forth a rod out of the stem of Jesse, and a Branch shall grow out of his roots:

(1) Spirit of the LORD,

(2) Spirit of wisdom,

(3) Spirit of understanding,

(4) Spirit of counsel,

(5) Spirit of power,

(6) Spirit of knowledge,

(7) Spirit of the fear of the Lord.

A few more examples of Angelic rank

Angels - type of angel closest to mankind who act as messengers; believed to be the same as guardian angels (Hebrews 1:14)

Archangels - "chief messengers" who are the primary messengers between God and mankind. (Jude 1:9)

Authorities - angels who bear authority (Col. 2:10)

Bene-Elohim - "sons of God" (Gen 6:`1-4)

Cherubim - second highest angels to God (Gen. 3:22-24)

Powers - sixth highest order of angels believed to be protectors of divine plans (Eph. 6:12)

Princes - high ranking angels equated with Archons and Principalities. **Principalities** - seventh highest order of angels who watch over the nations of the earth.   (Eph.   6:12)
Rulers - angels equated with Dominions and Principalities. (Eph 6:12)

Seraphim - angels highest and closest to God. (Isaiah 6:2) **Thrones** - third highest order of angels also called Seats.(Col. 1:16)

The Ante-chaotic Age

The Ante-chaotic Age - from the beginning of the original creation of the heavens and of the Earth (Genesis 1:1) to the flooded, chaotic state of the Earth after God's judgment on Lucifer's kingdom (Genesis 1:2; Psalm 104:6; Isaiah 14:12-14; Jeremiah 4:23-26).

The Ante-chaotic Age extended from the original creation of the heavens and the Earth and all things therein to the rebellion and overthrow of the first kosmos, or social order on the Earth.

It was the dateless period between Gen.1:1 when the Earth was finished and inhabited in the beginning and Gen.1:2 when the Earth was first flooded, destroying all life therein. It takes in that unknown time during which Earth was in its first perfect state and ruled by Lucifer before he rebelled and caused the Earth to be flooded, as in Gen. 1:2.

This is called the Gap Theory

Theory Defined: an idea or set of ideas that is intended to explain facts or events, an idea that is suggested or presented as possibly true but that is not known or proven to be true.

In studying and research you will find many debates over doctrine, history and events, for me one thing remains sure Christ is my redeemer and only means of Salvation.

As we study these difference subjects in light of Spiritual warfare I will use many facts, theories, doctrinal and historical biblical views based on the Bible and doctrines that are believed about spiritual warfare in the heavenly and early warfare.

Note: What do I feel about the Gap Theory or Dispensation of Angels I believe it is possible, even thou like many things in the Bible we will know more clearly when we stand before the Father in the Kingdom.

God did not create the earth a ruin and a waste.

The gap theory was another significant attempt by Christian theologians to reconcile the time scale of world history found in Genesis with the popular belief that geologists provide "undeniable" evidence that the world is exceedingly old (billions of years).

Thomas Chalmers (Courtesy of Films for Christ).

Thomas Chalmers (1780-1847), a notable Scottish theologian and first moderator of the Free Church of Scotland, was perhaps the man most responsible for the gap theory.[1] The idea can be traced back to the rather obscure writings of the Dutchman Episcopius (1583-1643), and was first recorded from one of Chalmers' lectures in 1814.[2] Rev. William Buckland, a geologist, did much to popularize the idea.

Although Chalmers' writings give very little information about the gap theory,[3] many of the details are obtained from other writers such as the 19th century geologist Hugh Miller, who quoted from Chalmers' lectures on the subject.[4]

his ruin-reconstruction view is held by many who use Bible study aids such as the Scofield Reference Bible, Dake's Annotated Reference Bible, and The Newberry Reference Bible.

Gen 1:1 In the beginning God created the Heaven and the earth.

Gen 1:2 And the earth was without form, and void; and darkness was upon the face of the deep. And the Spirit of God moved upon the face of the waters.

King James Bible

Isaiah 45: 18 For thus saith the LORD that created the heavens; God himself that formed the earth and made it; he hath established it, he created it not in vain, he formed it to be inhabited: I am the LORD; and there is none else.

Isaiah 45: 18 For thus says the LORD, who created the heavens (He is the God who formed the earth and made it, He established it and did not create it a waste place, but formed it to be inhabited), "I am the LORD, and there is none else.

Before we get into this verse, let's understand the Hebrew word used for "vain". In the Hebrew text the word is "tohu", and this is the same word as God gave in Genesis 1:2.

Genesis 1:2 "And the earth was without form, and void; and darkness was upon the face of the deep. And the Spirit of God moved upon the face of the waters."

The word "tohu" means void and without form. God is saying that He did not create the earth void and without form, but it became that way. "And the earth was" is also a phrase that we must take back to the Hebrew text, for the word "was" in the Hebrew text should read "became". In the Strong's Hebrew Dictionary, the number is 1961. "Hayah, haw-yaw', a prime root, to become, or come to pass, to cause to happen." The earth was not created "tohu" or without form and void, but became that way.

In Genesis 1:1; "In the beginning God created the heaven and the earth." This is a flat statement, and the purpose of His creation is given to us here in Isaiah 45:18; "He hath established it, He created it not in vain, He formed it to be inhabited:" He "established" it to give it order, and the purpose for establishing it was that it would be "inhabited." It was in that established place that the dinosaurs, and all the other creatures that are extinct today, roamed.

GOD FIRST GAVE ANGELS DOMINION OVER THE EARTH AND PLANETS

Gods original plan to populate earth with millions, maybe billions of angels backfired when they destroyed the planet and turned it into a dark evil wasteland. Lucifer was trained as a super arch angel to rule over the angels who where given the job of turning the world into a paradise.

Over millions of years lucifer, who thought he could dethrone the real God managed to turn the angels against him resulting in a dark evil chaos here on earth.

God cleaned up the mess, he created another paradise to be populated by humans but Adam and Eve failed their first test with Satan, who is still here and we can see the result all around us.

Angels inhabited this earth before the creation of man.

It is revealed in Isaiah 14 and Ezekiel 28, that God placed the archangel Lucifer, a cherub, on a throne on the earth. He was placed there as a ruler over the entire earth. God intended him to rule the earth by administering the government of God over the earth. And the government of God was administered on earth until the rebellion of the sinning angels.

How long these angels inhabited the earth before the creation of man is not revealed. It might have been millions--or even billions--of years. More on that later. But these angels sinned. Sin is the transgression of God's law (I John 3:4). And God's law is the basis of God's government. So we know these angels, apparently a third of all the angels (Rev. 12:4), sinned--rebelled against the government of God. And sin carries penalties.

The penalty for the sin of the angels is not death, as it is for man. Angels are immortal spirit beings and cannot die. These spirit beings had been given dominion over the PHYSICAL EARTH as a possession and an abode.

The universal, worldwide sin of the angels resulted in the physical destruction of the face of the earth.

Satan's fall from heaven is symbolically described in Isaiah 14:12-14 and Ezekiel 28:12-18. While these two passages are referring specifically to the kings of Babylon and Tyre, they also reference the spiritual power behind those kings, namely, Satan.

These passages describe why Satan fell, but they do not specifically say when the fall occurred. What we do know is this: the angels were created before the earth (Job 38:4-7).

Satan fell before he tempted Adam and Eve in the Garden (Genesis 3:1-14). Satan's fall, therefore, must have occurred somewhere after the time the angels were created and before he tempted Adam and Eve in the Garden of Eden.

Whether Satan's fall occurred a few minutes, hours, or days before he tempted Adam and Eve in the Garden, Scripture does not specifically say.

The book of Job tells us, at least at that time, Satan still had access to heaven and to the throne of God. "One day the angels came to present themselves before the LORD, and Satan also came with them. The LORD said to Satan, 'Where have you come from?'

Satan answered the LORD, 'From roaming through the earth and going back and forth in it'" (Job 1:6-7). Apparently at that time, Satan was still moving freely between heaven and earth, speaking to God directly and answering for his activities. At what point God discontinued this access is unknown.

Why did Satan fall from heaven? Satan fell because of pride. He desired to be God, not to be a servant of God. Notice the many "I will..." statements in Isaiah 14:12-15. Ezekiel 28:12-15 describes Satan as an exceedingly beautiful angel.

Satan was likely the highest of all angels, the most beautiful of all of God's creations, but he was not content in his position. Instead, Satan desired to be God, to essentially "kick God off His throne" and take over the rule of the universe. Satan wanted to be God, and interestingly enough, that is what Satan tempted Adam and Eve with in the Garden of Eden (Genesis 3:1-5). How did Satan fall from heaven?

Actually, a fall is not an accurate description. It would be far more accurate to say God cast Satan out of heaven (Isaiah 14:15; Ezekiel 28:16-17). Satan did not fall from heaven; rather, Satan was pushed out of heaven.

Now Lucifer did not just up and decided that he would dethrone God, Lucifer was full of wisdom he stood in the presence of God. He knew there was no way he could dethrone God, his desire was to be like the Most High, he lust after the throne that Jesus occupied.

There was war in heaven, if what I believe is true, than earth was already in existence and indeed part of heaven when this war took place that war that started in heaven continued on earth destroying the original earth.

Remember that during this war the faithful angels of the lord imprisoned many of the angels of Satan. Now, ask yourself where is that prison that the rebels are locked away in? There's no doubt that that prison is in the heart of the earth!

Those in prison in the heart of the earth are prisoners of war [POW's.]Now in order for there to be prisoners jailed in the heart of the earth before man was created, there must have been war in the earth before man was created.

This war is what destroyed the original creation and caused the earth to become formless and a chaotic mass of darkness when the Spirit of the Lord hovered above the earth to recreate and prepare it for his new creation, man. God did not created this world as a chaotic mass, it fell into that state as the result of war the between the angels of Satan and the angels the Lord. That war in the earth never ended it continues to this day, a new combatant was just introduced, the man.

The Dispensation of Angels Highlighted

The Antechaotic Age (Genesis 1:1-2):

1. Name. We call it the dispensation of angels, because angels were given rulership under God to administer His will and rule the earth and other planets (Isaiah 14:12-14; Ezekiel 28:11-17; Matthew 25:41; Ephes. 1:21; Ephes. 3:9-10; Ephes. 6:12; Col. 1:15-18; 1 Peter 3:22; Rev. 12:7-10; Rev. 20:10).

2. Length-from the time the earth was created in the presence of angels (Job 38:4-7) to the time of chaos and defeat of Satan in his invasion of heaven (Genesis 1:2; Isaiah 14:12-14; Ezekiel 28:11-17; Luke 10:18).

3. Favorable beginning. Every angel, devil, and person was sinless to begin with (Ephes. 1:21; Ephes. 3:9-10; Col. 1:15-18; 1 Peter 3:22). Lucifer, the ruling cherub of earth, is described as "perfect in thy ways from the day that thou was created, till iniquity was found in thee" (Ezekiel 28:11-17).

This scripture and Isaiah 14:12-14 picture his exalted position. He had a most favorable beginning and it would have remained so had he not exalted himself in an effort to dethrone God (Ezekiel 28:17; 1 Tim. 3:6).

4. Test. The test for angelic rulers was the same as for man-to obey Him in all that He commanded. Lucifer had ways to walk in (Ezekiel 28:15), and so did all other angels, or they could not have sinned. Sin is transgression of the law for angels as well as human beings (1 John 3:4).

5. Purpose of God. His purpose was to test angels to see if they would remain true to Him before using them eternally as trusted servants. For this same reason God tested man, His purpose for testing being alike for all free moral and responsible agents. Satan and others failed because they "abode not in the truth" (John 8:44; Ephes. 3:9-10; 1 Tim. 5:21; 1 John 5:18-19; 2 Peter 2:4; Jude 1:6-7).

6. The means of God in accomplishing His purpose. God used the ways that He restricted the angels to walk in as the means of testing them (Ezekiel 28:15; John 8:44; Ephes. 3:9-10).

7. Failure. Some angelic beings failed to continue in the truth (John 8:44) and the ways which God made clear to them (Ezekiel 28:11-17). Over one-third rebelled, including Lucifer who will be cast down to earth with the other rebellious angels in the middle of the future tribulation (Rev. 12:4,7-12). God found it necessary to charge them with folly (Job 4:18), sin (2 Peter 2:4; Jude 1:6-7), and rebellion (Isaiah 14:12-14; Ezekiel 28:11-17; Rev. 12:7-12).

8. Judgment for sin. God prepared hell "for the devil and his angels" (Matthew 25:41). Some are in hell now (2 Peter 2:4; Jude 1:6-7). Lucifer and those still loose with him will eventually be put into hell (Matthew 25:41; Rev. 12:7-12; Rev. 20:10). Immediate judgment came by their defeat and God taking away their rulership (Isaiah 14:12-14; Ezekiel 28:11-17).

They would not be rulers of earth now Adam, the new ruler of the earth, had not fallen and submitted to them (Genesis 3:1-24; Romans 5:12-21; Ephes. 2:1-3; Ephes. 4:27; Ephes. 6:1; 1 John 5:18-19; Rev. 12:9-12). Now, in Christ, man has power over them (Ephes. 6:10-18; James 4:7; 1 Peter 5:7-9) and will eventually have the entire dominion restored to him (Psalm 8; Daniel 7:18,27; Hebrews 2:9-18; Rev. 5:10; Rev. 20:4-6; Rev. 22:4-6).

JUDGEMENT OF THE FALLEN ONES

(2 Pet 2:4 KJV) For if God spared not the angels that sinned, but cast them down to hell, and delivered them into chains of darkness, to be reserved unto judgment;

The Greek word "Tartarus" is only found once in the whole Bible. Tartarus describes the place, where a specific group of fallen angels are held until the final judgment. The verb tartaroo, translated "cast down to hell" in 2 Pet. 2:4, signifies to consign to Tartarus, which is neither Sheol nor hades nor hell, but the place where those angels whose special sin is referred to in that passage are confined "to **be reserved unto judgment;"** the region is described as "pits of darkness," RV.

2 Peter 2:4 NKJV™
For if God did not spare the angels who sinned, but cast [them] down to hell and delivered [them] into chains of darkness, to be reserved for judgment;

This verse says that "the angels that sinned"(which would include Lucifer, too) have already been cast down "to hell" by God Himself. Yet they aren't burning right now, obviously, and they certainly aren't suffering somewhere far beneath the earth. **Tartarus means "dark abyss" or "place of restraint."** It isn't a place of punishment either. Look carefully. 2 Peter 2:4 says Satan's angels are "**reserved unto judgment," which means their punishment is yet future.** For Satan and his evil angels, the fire hasn't started yet.

Jude 1:6 NKJV™
And the angels who did not keep their proper domain, but left their own abode, **He has reserved in everlasting chains under darkness for the judgment of the great day;**

Mat 25:41 Then shall he say also unto them on the left hand, Depart from me, ye cursed, into everlasting fire, prepared for the devil and his angels:

The Five Compartments of Hell

The word of God speaks of five different compartments of Hell. Knowing these compartments will help us to understand more about Hell and rightly divide the Scriptures on this subject. Many people have taken Scriptures out of their context and have created a false doctrine on the subject of Hell.

What are the five compartments of Hell?

1.) Tartarus

2.) Abraham's Bosom (The Paradise of old)

3.) Hades or Sheol

4.) The Abyss (Bottomless Pit)

5.) The Lake of Fire (Gehenna)

Tartarus-

Tartarus is the Greek form of the word Hell. It is the compartment where fallen angels are kept, reserved in chains of darkness until they are judged by God and cast into the final Hell, the Lake of Fire (II Peter 2:4, Jude 1:6).

"For if God spared not the angles that sinned, but cast them down to Hell (Tartarus), and delivered them into chains of darkness, to be reserved unto judgment;"(II Peter 2:4)

Abraham's Bosom

Abraham's Bosom is the place referred to as the Paradise of old. It was the compartment where all the righteous dead of the Old Testament were kept. There was no torment or suffering in Abraham's Bosom. It was simply a place of holding until the death and resurrection of Jesus. Jesus paid the price by shedding His blood. At the resurrection of Jesus, Abraham's Bosom was emptied and removed from the heart of the earth and is now located in heaven. All the captives were set free and resurrected (Matthew 27:51-53). The account of Abraham's Bosom is found in the **Gospel of Luke, chapter 16 verses 19-31.**

"And it came to pass, that the beggar died, and was carried by the angles into Abraham's Bosom: the rich man also died, and was buried."(Luke 16:22, 23, 25).

"And in Hell he lift up his eyes, being in torment, and seeth Abraham afar off, and Lazarus in his bosom."

(Luke 16:23).

"But Abraham said, Son, remember that thou in thy lifetime receivedst thy good things, and likewise Lazarus evil things: but now he is comforted, and thou art tormented."

(Luke 16:25).

Hades or Sheol

This is the place for the wicked after death. When the sinner dies, his spirit and soul go immediately to this place of torment.

The term Hades is the Greek form of the word Hell. **The definition of the word Hades is as follows: the place (or state) of departed souls; the grave; Hell.**

Because the word grave is mentioned in the definition of Hades, it is said by some that Hell is the common grave; and from this, the doctrine of soul sleep is derived. My friend, Hades is more than the common grave. The rich man of Luke chapter 16 was in Hades and his soul was not asleep; it was in much turmoil.

The term Sheol is the Hebrew word for Hell. In the Hebrew language the word Sheol is defined as: Hades or the world of the dead (as is a subterranean retreat).

Hades or Sheol are the Greek and Hebrew terms for the word "Hell." Don't let those who try to impress you with theological terms **throw you off track and teach you that Hell is just the common grave.** Note some Scriptures where they are used:

1.) Hades - Luke 16:23; Revelation 20:13.

2.) Sheol - Isaiah 14:9; Psalm 9:17.

The Abyss

Rev 20:3 And cast him into the bottomless pit, and shut him up, and set a seal upon him, that he should deceive the nations no more, till the thousand years should be fulfilled: and after that he must be loosed a little season.

This place is also known by the name "The Bottomless Pit." This compartment of Hell is where Satan will be bound for 1,000 years during the reign of Christ on earth (Revelation 20:1-7).

Also during the time of the Great Tribulation period, it will be where the locust-like scorpion creatures will come and torment mankind for five months, (Revelation 9:1-11). The Abyss will not be the eternal home of Satan. He will be loosed from this prison to be judged, then cast into the eternal Hell, the Lake of Fire forever, (Revelation 20:10).

The Lake of Fire

The Lake of Fire is the eternal home of all sin and rebellion. Another name for this place is called "Gehenna." At the close of the White Throne Judgment of God, this will be the home of the wicked (Revelation 20:11-15). The Lake of Fire will be the home of those who rebelled against God. There fallen man will be, for all eternity, to suffer the pains of an eternal Hell.

Satan will be there for all eternity to suffer also. According to the Scripture, Satan will be tormented day and night forever and ever, having no rest.

Also, Hades and Sheol will be cast into the eternal Hell. Those who inhabit Hades and Sheol will be resurrected to face God's Judgement, then cast into the Lake of Fire. In the very end of God's judgements, the wicked, Satan, fallen angels and sin will have their home in the Lake of Fire.

The Spirit, Soul, and Body in Hell

The Apostle Paul, in his letter to the Thessalonians, exhorted his brethren and prayed that God would sanctify them wholly and that their spirit, soul and body would be preserved blameless unto the coming of our Lord Jesus Christ, (I Thessalonians 5:23).

Paul's prayer was that the total man be saved. Many think that once you die, that's it, but not so. Some even think that their physical body will not feel the fires of Hell. The truth of the matter is that, when men are cast into the eternal Hell (the Lake of Fire) they will be cast as a total, complete and physical man.

When an unrighteous man dies, his spirit and soul are separated from his body. His body goes back to the dust of the earth, and his spirit and soul go to Hades and Sheol to be tormented there until the White Throne Judgment of God. Many think that the body will stay forever in the dust (grave) of the earth.

The Word of God declares that those who sleep in the dust of the earth shall awake, some to everlasting life and some to everlasting shame and contempt (Daniel 12:2).

Another account states that those that are in the graves shall hear God's voice, those that have done good and those that have done evil. The righteous awake to everlasting life, and the wicked awake to everlasting damnation (John 5:28, 29).

There is coming a time when the lost will be physically resurrected to face God. In the eternal Hell, man will be in his physical, resurrected body to face the pains of Hell. Paul's prayer was that you be preserved blameless spirit, soul and body. Men that die without Jesus will be judged spirit, soul and body.

The reason for this total judgment of man is because on earth man sinned in his total body. God will judge the total man. Many try to reason and figure in their mind how the physical body of a man can stand the eternal flames of Hell and not die or be destroyed?'

The Word of God speaks of the judgment of the last enemy called death (I Corinthians 15:26). The Spirit of death will be cast into the Lake of Fire

(Revelation 20:14). When death is cast into the Lake of Fire, the power of death will be broken.

Death will no longer be able to touch man after his resurrection, man will never die again; and since death only affects the body, man will live in the eternal flames of Hell in his physical body forever. Just think of it...man in his body will burn forever.

Have you ever been burned before? Think of that being multiplied many, many times all over your entire body forever. Please give your life to Jesus today.

Hell will not be a house party, as some would like to believe. Hell, my friend, is a serious place of eternal judgment for all that are lost. Note other Scriptures that declare the resurrection of the dead: Isaiah 26:19; Hosea 13:14; Acts 24:15.

The Scriptural Mandate on Hell

Throughout our study of Hell, we have given you what the Word of God teaches on the subject. I hope now that you can see the reality of this place of judgment on sin. We have not shunned to give you the whole counsel of God. Now let's go back to see the scriptural mandate given in this study.

1.) We learned that Hell will be a place of pain and sorrow for the lost, (Luke 16:19-31).

2.) We learned that Hell was created by God and not the devil, (Matthew 25:41).

3.) We noted that the flames of Hell are forever and will never burn out, (Mark 9:43-48; Isaiah 66:24; Matthew 12:8).

4.) We saw those who are candidates for this place, (Psalm 9:17; Proverbs 7:5-25; Revelation 21:8).

5.) We learned about the five compartments of Hell: (1) Tartarus (2) Abraham's Bosom (3) Hades or Sheol (4) The Abyss (5) The Lake of Fire.

6.) We learned that the sinner's complete body will be in Hell's fire, never to die or to be physically destroyed, (after his resurrection and judgment at God's White Throne.) (Revelation 20:11-15; John 5:28, 29).

THE FALL OF MAN AND THE WARFARE OF THE MIND

Gen 3:14 And the Lord God said unto the serpent, Because thou hast done this, thou art cursed above all cattle, and above every beast of the field; upon thy belly shalt thou go, and dust shalt thou eat all the days of thy life: SERPENT ONCE WALKED UPRIGHT

Gen 3:15 And I will put enmity between thee and the woman, and between thy seed and her seed; it shall bruise thy head, and thou shalt bruise his heel.

The events following the Judgment of a seed that would bruise the Serpent head is why Stan has worked so hard to kill the seed to come Christ Jesus himself.

Satan and his demons had no way of knowing for sure who the redeemer would be so he went about attacking the son and daughters of Adam and Eve.

UNDERSTANDING THE WARFARE OF THE MIND

Satan took his war against God to a new battlefront – the heart of man. He tempted Adam and Eve to sin (Gen 3:1) which led to man being spiritually separated from God. (Rom 6:23)

As Satan's time runs short he and his demons increase their activity. (Rev 12:12) These activities involve opposing the plan of God (Dan 10:13) and leading people away from Christ. (1 Cor 10:20)

They appeal to man's spiritual desires by disguising themselves as "angels of light" (2 Cor 11:14), seducing many with wicked doctrine, (1 Tim 4:1) and drawing them into a form of godliness which has no power to save. (2 Tim 3:5)

Demons can sometimes afflict people with various physical conditions (Matt 9:33; Mark 5:2-16) though it's very important to note that Scripture distinguishes between natural and demonic illness (Matt 4:24; Mrk 1:32). They attempt to delay the answers to godly prayer (Dan 10:13) and draw nations into war (Rev 16:14).

Demons attempt to snare believers in sin (1 Tim 3:7). When they sin, Satan acts as their accuser (Rev 12:10).

The Mind in its original creation was perfect after God's images:

Gen 1:27 So God created man in his own image, in the image of God created he him; male and female created he them. KJV

Own Image Defined: OT:6754 resemblance; hence, a representative figure and likeness.

- Mind was uncorrupted
- Heart or Soul was not evil
- They had a sound mind
- Single Mind
- Peaceful Mind
- Creative Mind
- Steadfast Mind
- Retentive Mind

In order to bind mankind the serpent went after mankind's mind through the souls.

Soul Defined:

"Soul" is a religious term but it includes our mind, from which we derive our thoughts, our mentality, and our heart.

The soul is in constant interaction with your body.

For example, the physical body letss us know when it's hungry and craves certain tastes.

These signals are sent to the brain and the mind tries to work out a solution to answer that need. A more developed mind can overcome the immediate desires of the body in favor of long-term health.

There are the parts of our mind that deal with daily life decisions, but there are also the deeper parts of our soul that deal more with our higher level subconscious self. This part of ourselves becomes fully active when our body sleeps and reaches the dream state.

THE FALL SEATED THE MIND IN THE PLACE OF THE SPIRIT OF A MAN!

Prov 20:27 The spirit of man is the candle of the Lord, searching all the inward parts of the belly. KJV

Gen 3:2- And the woman said unto the serpent, We may eat of the fruit of the trees of the garden:

Gen 3:3 But of the fruit of the tree which is in the midst of the garden, God hath said, Ye shall not eat of it, neither shall ye touch it, lest ye die.

Gen 3:4 And the serpent said unto the woman, Ye shall not surely die:

Gen 3:5 For God doth know that in the day ye eat thereof, then your eyes shall be opened, and ye shall be as gods, knowing good and evil.

- Convince mankind that God really didn't mean what he said, not to you (Ye shall not surely die:)

- You are your own god, captain of your destiny, self made man or woman (ye shall be as gods,)

- You determine what right or wrong because after all you smart, educated, well learned, successful. (ye shall be as gods, knowing good and evil.)

Gen 3:5 And when the woman saw that the tree was good for food, and that it was pleasant to the eyes, and a tree to be desired to make one wise, she took of the fruit thereof, and did eat, and gave also unto her husband with her; and he did eat.

- They used the appetite, cravings and addiction to enter mankind – (tree was good for food)

- Next they appealed to her visual pleasure, through the eye gate – (pleasant to the eyes)

- To get rooted in mankind real good these spirits road in on their desires it became their guide, thus the ground was wide open to them now to enter mankind.
-

Gen 3:6 And when the woman saw that the tree was good for food, and that it was pleasant to the eyes, and a tree to be desired to make one wise, she took of the fruit thereof, and did eat, and gave also unto her husband with her; and he did eat.

1 John 2:16 For all that is in the world, the lust of the flesh, and the lust of the eyes, and the pride of life, is not of the Father, but is of the world. KJV

- Lust of the Eyes – Pleasant or Pleasure
- Lust of the Flesh – Desire
- Pride of Life – Make wise Knowable puffed up with pride

Gen 3:10-11 – After the fall the mind begin to rule man filling him with guilt and self conscienceless.

Gen 3:10 And he said, I heard thy voice in the garden, and I was afraid, because I was naked; and I hid myself.

Gen 3:11 And he said, Who told thee that thou wast naked? Hast thou eaten of the tree, whereof I commanded thee that thou shouldest not eat?

When looking carefully at Paul's statement about the deception of Eve you can easily see how deception can not only effect the carnal mind but by long term effect become a gate way to demonic bondage.

2 Cor 11:3 But I fear, lest by any means, as the serpent beguiled Eve through his subtlety, so your minds should be corrupted from the simplicity that is in Christ.

2 Cor 11:4 For if he that cometh preacheth another Jesus, whom we have not preached, or if ye receive another spirit, which ye have not received, or another gospel, which ye have not accepted, ye might well bear with him.

Deception can open the door to a believer becoming bound by an evil spirit, depending on the degree of deception and yielding their life over to the deceptive spirits. Paul, while talking to the Spirit filled Corinthian church, warned them of receiving another spirit.

Many honest, well meaning people, sinners and saints, have been bound by deception, opening the door to satanic bondage and a grave need for deliverance from being captive to a deceiving spirit.

COUNTERFEIT MANIFESTATIONS

2 Cor 11:14 And no marvel; for Satan himself is transformed into an angel of light.

It is of the utmost importance that every believer understand that the enemy of our soul will pretend that he is God, Jesus, or the Holy Spirit when it suits his plan of deception. This statement is true in respect to the fact that the Bible teaches that there are false apostles, false prophets, false teachers, false pastors or shepherds, and of no doubt false evangelists. These all carry with them spirits that can and will transfer as a counterfeit manifestation of the spirit of God using them.

The first thing that the enemy must do is keep the deceived believer thinking that every time they have a leading, it is the Spirit of God giving it to them, not realizing that a believer can operate under dual leadings and, if not judged, they will accept a revelation from Satan, thinking that it is God. A good example of this is Peter (Matthew 16:13-17, 21-23) when he, by the Spirit of God, had revelation that Jesus "was the Christ" and a few verses later, he spoke by Satan that Jesus was not to be crucified.

The church is literally loaded with dual manifestations operating un-judged and un-discerned because of a false safety net that gives the impression that once you are saved and spirit filled, it is not possible that Satan could speak through you, when that is just not true.

TRUE AND COUNTERFEIT ACCEPTED TOGETHER

Briefly put, this is a glimpse into the mixed "manifestations" which have come upon the Church of God, since the Revival in Wales; for, almost without exception, in every land where revival has since broken forth, within a very brief period of time the counterfeit stream has mingles with the true; and almost without exception, true and false have been accepted together, because of the workers being ignorant of the possibility of concurrent streams; or else have been rejected together by those who could not detect the one from the other; or it has been believed that there was no "true" at all, because the majority of believers fail to understand that there can be mixed workings of the (1) Divine and Satanic, (2) Divine and human, (3) Satanic and human, (4) soul and spirit, (5) soul and body, (6) body and spirit; the three latter in the way of feelings and consciousness, and the three former in the way of source and power. (War On The Saints, Unabridged Edition, by Jessie Penn-Lewis, pp 99-100).

1. The preaching of Another Jesus: Another Jesus is not the Lord Jesus Christ being ministered to the hearer but a Spirit of Anti-Christ being taught as Jesus and the deceived victim opens their spirit man up to an evil spirit called Another Jesus or Anti-Christ. Without being critical, I have met many believers who go to churches that are preaching another Jesus and the entire congregation are manifesting the same spirit of anti-Christ.

Testimony: *While praying for a number of people coming through a prayer line, a lady came through screaming, "Jesus, Jesus, Jeeesusss", with a hissing sound. I recognized that this was another Jesus not the Lord Jesus Christ being called upon. When I said to the Lady, "Which Jesus?", she started cursing me out and called me an S.O.B. and how dare you challenge me. I cast it out and God set her free.*

2. Receiving another Spirit: When a believer or sinner receives something operating in their life that they think is God and is not, they stand a chance of receiving another spirit. The danger in this is that the deceived person will fight to hold on to the manifestation of what they consider the Holy Spirit when it is not. Religious spirits have a ball living in the minds and honest hearts of deceived people, sinner or saint.

Religious Spirits Manifestations (Religious but not saved): One type of religious spirit will have a person believing in God but never accepting Jesus Christ as Lord. They will even go so far as to pray, but never become born again by confessing their sins to Jesus and asking him to become their Lord and Saviour. This type of deceived person is yet in their sins and will die and go to hell if they don't repent.

All this is done to open the victim up to another spirit. This type of person even prides themselves on how the Lord blesses them, but never serves the one they confess as blessing them. Satan does this by blinding their mind so they will not give their life to the Lord (II Corinthians 4:3-4).

3. Another Gospel: A Gospel inspired by Spirit of Error, causing the deceived believer to depart from the true faith, giving heed to a Seducing Spirits and Doctrines of Devils.

1 Tim 4:1 Now the Spirit speaketh expressly, that in the latter times some shall depart from the faith, giving heed to seducing spirits, and doctrines of devils;

The Basic Principles For Testing Teachings By Teaching Spirits

Since thought, or "belief," originates either from the God of Truth, or the father of lies (John 8:44), there is but one basic principle for testing the source of all doctrine, or "thoughts" and "beliefs," held by believers, or unbelievers, i.e., the test of the revealed Word of God. All "truth" is in harmony with the only channel of revealed truth in the world - the written Word of God. All "teachings" originating from deceiving spirits-

1. Weaken the authority of the Scriptures;

2. Distort the teaching in the Scriptures;

3. Add to the Scriptures the thoughts of men;or

4. Put the Scriptures entirely aside.

Jessie Penn-Lewis tells how spirit operates once they gain a foothold (War On The Saints, Unabridged Edition, by Jessie Penn-Lewis, page 21).

A. Counterfeit dreams and visions

B. Counterfeiting the peace of God

C. Counterfeit feelings of joy

D. Counterfeit voices

E. Counterfeit angelic visitations

F. Counterfeit spirits on the body frame

G. Counterfeit guidance's

H. Counterfeit of the human spirit

I. Counterfeit self condemnation

J. Counterfeit sin

K. Counterfeit tongues (false tongues)

L. Counterfeit oratory spirits

M. Counterfeit blaspheming the Holy Ghost

N. Counterfeit love

O. Counterfeiting the Gifts of the Spirit

P. Counterfeiting the five-fold ministries

Q. Counterfeit leadings

"You don't do what you do because you have a demon you often get demons because of what you have been doing" By Apostle Ivory Hopkins

THE WORD MAKES IT CLEAR A SPIRITS ENTERED MANKIND THROUGH DISOBEDIENCE

Eph 2:2 Wherein in time past ye walked according to the course of this world, according to the prince of the power of the air, the spirit that now worketh in the children of disobedience:

Gen 4:1-7 - Cain's Parents open the door to the carnal mind and his act open the door to the demonic realm. The death of Abel was related to stopping the Holy seed.

Gen 4:1 And Adam knew Eve his wife; and she conceived, and bare Cain, and said, I have gotten a man from the Lord.

Gen 4:2 And she again bare his brother Abel. And Abel was a keeper of sheep, but Cain was a tiller of the ground.

Gen 4:3 And in process of time it came to pass, that Cain brought of the fruit of the ground an offering unto the Lord.

Gen 4:4 And Abel, he also brought of the firstlings of his flock and of the fat thereof. And the Lord had respect unto Abel and to his offering:

Gen 4:5 But unto Cain and to his offering he had not respect. And Cain was very wroth, and his countenance fell.

Gen 4:6 And the Lord said unto Cain, Why art thou wroth? and why is thy countenance fallen?

Gen 4:7 If thou doest well, shalt thou not be accepted? and if thou doest not well, **sin lieth at the** door. And **unto thee shall be his desire**, and **thou shalt rule over him.**

Sin in this verse is seen as a noun a word (other than a pronoun) used to identify any of a class of people, places, or things.

- **sin lieth at the door**
- **unto thee shall be his desire**
- **thou shalt rule over him.**

Scholars have long noted the grammatical difficulties and awkward translation of the Hebrew in Genesis 4:7.

The ambiguities are removed by viewing the Hebrew word *robes* (translated as "crouching"), not as a participle modifying the term "sin," but as an Akkadian loan word *rabisum*, which means "demon."

From this perspective, the translation of Genesis 4:7 becomes:

If you do well, will not your countenance be lifted up? And if you do not do well, sin is *a demon* at the door; and its [the demon's] desire is for you, but you must master it [the demon].

Some scholars view Genesis 4:7, taken with 1 John 3:12's characterization of Cain as "of the evil one," as suggesting the possibility that Cain was inhabited by a demon during his rebellion against God.

1 John 3:11-12 For this is the message that ye heard from the beginning, that we should love one another.

1 John 3:12 **Not as Cain, who was of that wicked one, and slew his brother**. And wherefore slew he him? Because his own works were evil, and his brother's righteous

What an amazing description. It waits to catch us…it's pictured as a demon crouching at the door, ready to trip us, and trap us.

Yet, Cain can be its master, and so can we.

God gave Cain a clear warning of the danger he was in and told him how to avoid the crouching demon at the door of his heart. He said… "Do right …and you will be accepted."

By looking at other translation of these verses you will see that spirits were directly involved in the murder of Cain's killing of Abel.

(This was brought my attention through Murell F. Ungers Author of Ungers Bible Dictionary and What Demons Can Do To Saints)

A. <u>Genesis 4:5-7</u>, New English Bible

"The Lord received Abel and his gift with favor; But Cain and his gift the Lord did not receive. Cain was very angry and his face fell.

Then the Lord said to Cain, Why are you so angry and cast down? If you do well you are accepted; if not **SIN OPENING THE DOOR TO DEMONS** crouching at the door. It shall be eager for you, and you will be mastered by it".

One of the earliest uses occurs in Genesis 6:4 "So the LORD said to Cain: "Why are you so resentful and crest fallen?

If you do well, you can hold up your head; **but if not, sin is a demon crouching** at your door; its urge is to enter into you, **yet you can be his master".**

The spectacular statement made by God regarding sin: 'yet you can be his master', is one of the most striking statements in spiritual warfare.

Then the Lord spoke to Cain in his solitude, "Why are you so angry? Why is your face dark with rage?

If you do right, will you not be accepted and exalted? But if you do not, sin is at your door. It desires to have you, but you can be its master."

We would do well then to take a lesson from God's fatherly words to Cain. As with Adam and Eve, and with Cain, sin is like a crouching demon that lies in wait for us, seeking dominion over our lives. As God said, *"Its urge is toward you, yet you can be its master"* (Genesis 4:7b, JT).

Before I go any further, I would like to quote from a mighty man of God, who has gone on with the Lord, H. A. Maxwell Whyte, from his book "Demons and Deliverance", page 97-98:

1. Can a Christian be possessed by a demon?

The very phrasing of this question is unfortunate. The question is usually asked in a derogatory manner by those who totally reject the idea that a born-again Christian could ever be troubled or afflicted by a demon.
The problem revolves around the use of the word possessed, a word that suggests the demon totally inhabits and owns the sufferer with no area free and with free will absolutely blocked.

I do not believe a born-again Christian can be possessed by a demon. The very idea of a Christian who loves the Lord being owned and controlled by a demon is totally abhorrent and unacceptable.

If Christians would abandon the use of this confusing word "possessed," and speak of demon problems in terms of "oppressions," "vexations," or "bindings," believers would avoid a lot of confusion.

HOW DO YOU MASTER SIN OPENING DOORS TO DEMONS

God's words to Cain remind us of Jesus' words to Peter: *"Simon, Simon, behold, Satan hath desired to have you, that he may sift you as wheat"* (Luke 22:31).

Was it not this same Peter who later said, *"Be sober, be vigilant; because your adversary the devil, as a roaring lion, walketh about, seeking whom he may desire.*

Whom resist stedfast in the faith, knowing that the same afflictions are accomplished in your brethren that are in the world"? (I Peter 5:8-9).

Eph 4:26 Be ye angry, and sin not: let not the sun go down upon your wrath:

Eph 4:27 Neither give place to the devil.

Paul warned the believers in Ephesians 4:27, "Neither give place to the devil." Also, 2 Corinthians 2:11 tells us, "Lest Satan should get an advantage of us: for we are not ignorant of his devices."

James 4:7 Submit yourselves therefore to God. Resist the devil, and he will flee from you.

If you've given the enemy rights to your soul or body, then you are up for a spiritual infection that can result in demonic bondage. There are certain sins and things that a person can do, which can defile (make unclean) the person. When a person is defiled, they are unclean and therefore vulnerable to a spiritual infection, and the 'germs' in this realm are demons.

Satan lies in wait. He afflicts. He "crouches at the door." As we go out into the world, he stalks his prey with relentless determination, like a hungry lion.

30 WAYS TO KEEP YOUR MIND IN PERFECT PEACE

By: Permission Dr. Bishop Jackie Green

2 Cor 10:5 Casting down imaginations, and every high thing that exalteth itself against the knowledge of God, and bringing into captivity every thought to the obedience of Christ;

2 Cor 10:6 And having in a readiness to revenge all disobedience, when your obedience is fulfilled.

Note from Apostle Ivory Hopkins: Every stronghold is effected by in the battlefield of the mind to merely think it's all demons only would be Biblically unbalanced and dangerous to both the teacher and one needing deliverance.

1. Mind your business and don't be a busy body. Tend to your own house.
2. Don't be habitually late or tardy. This adds additional stress and strain.
3. Forgiveness must be your first recourse and way of life
4. Be content with what you have, not jealous of others
5. Don't be anxious about the troubles and problems of tomorrow
6. Watch what comes out of your mouth. Speak truth and not lies.
7. Do not overspend your budget but try to manage your money well
8. Meditate daily on the Word of God
9. Study the Word daily for spiritual growth
10. Pray with your understanding and in tongues every day
11. Don't leave your mind vacant and thoughts wandering in your mind
12. Refuse to worry or have anxiety about anything
13. Keep away from evil and cast down vain imaginations
14. Don't put evil before your eyes. Be careful what you think and look upon.
15. Denounce and keep away from lust, perversion and pornography
16. Don't gossip and don't listen to gossipers
17. Rebuke and renounce occult involvement

18. Think positive thoughts and think on spiritual things (things above)

19. Value and organize your time daily; don't be a time waster

20. Don't procrastinate but get it done

21. Meditate on the Word of God, not the problem

22. Memorize the Word of God

23. Read and sing the Word of God to yourself

24. Prophesy and speak the Word and declare the Word and not doubt

25. Pray over your mind and cover your dreams each night in prayer

26. Get proper rest and power naps

27. Refresh your mind daily with praise and worship unto the Lord

28. Laugh and smile daily

29. Relax and have some fun

38 Types of Minds Found in Scripture OLD TESTAMENT

By: Permission Dr. Bishop Jackie Green

1. **A Stayed Mind - Isaiah 26:3**
2. **A Mind to Work- Nehemiah 4:6**
3. **Out of Mind- Psalms 31:12**
4. **Recalling Mind- Lamentations 3:21**
5. **Willing Mind- I Chronicles 28:9**
6. **Alienated Mind- Ezekiel 23:17-18**
7. **Set Mind- Ezekiel 24:25**
8. **Despiteful Mind- Ezekiel 36:5**
9. **Mind of the Lord- Leviticus 24:12**
10. **Foolish Mind- Proverbs 29:11**
11. **Hardened Mind- Daniel 5:20**
12. **Changed Mind- Habakkuk 1:11**
13. **Grieving Mind- Genesis 26:35**
14. **Chafed Mind- II Samuel 17:8**
15. **Sorrowing Mind- Deuteronomy 28: 65**

NEW TESTAMENT
By: Permission Dr. Bishop Jackie Green

1. **Pure Mind– I Peter 3:1**
2. **Blinded Mind- II Corinthians 3:14**
3. **Corrupt Mind– II Corinthians 11:3**
4. **Reprobate Mind– Romans 1:28**
5. **Mind of Christ– I Corinthians 2:16**
6. **Vain Mind– Ephesians 4:17**
7. **Renewed Mind– Ephesians 4:23**
8. **Fleshly Mind– Colossians 2:18**
9. **Shaken Mind– II Thessalonians 2:2**
10. **Double Mind– James 1:8**
11. **Defiled Mind- Titus 1:15**
12. **Sober Mind– Titus 2:6**
13. **High Minded– II Timothy 3:4**
14. **Spiritually Minded– Romans 8:6**
15. **Carnal Minded– Romans 8:6-7**
16. **Wise Mind– Revelation 17:9**
17. **Evil Minds– Acts 14:2**
18. **Weary/Faint Minds– Hebrews 12**

Deliverance Team Care In the Local Church

Luke 10:1 After these things the Lord appointed other seventy also, and sent them two and two before his face into every city and place, whither he himself would come.

Luke 10:2 Therefore said he unto them, The harvest truly is great, but the labourers are few: pray ye therefore the Lord of the harvest, that he would send forth labourers into his harvest.

1. The pastor and church leadership must believe in the ministry of Jesus Christ and the importance of deliverance for themselves and the church. There can be no real "Deliverance Team" without pastoral approval.

2. A deliverance ministry in the local church must have a pastor that understands deliverance, cast out devils, is able to train and impart to the team. The pastor must be transparent and apt to demonstrate it in the church. Deliverance Team members must first go through ongoing deliverance themselves. They can practice on one another.

3. Training is very important for the team. Connecting with other anointed ministries that are moving in the ministry of deliverance is a great way to learn.

4. Persons who are "solo mentality" do not work well on such a team. Jesus' pattern was team ministry, and two by two. Husbands and wives on a team are ideal as well.

5. Conflict and personal issues on a Deliverance Team will be used to Satan's advantage. A Deliverance Team must constantly check themselves for un forgiveness, offense and sins on the team.

Deliverance is an ongoing process even for the team. Deal with team conflict quickly! Sit down or sit out if issues remain not dealt with. "Contamination unchecked" destroys deliverance ministry.

Deliverance Team members must be humble, knowledgeable in the Word, strong prayer and fasting lifestyle, a keen sense of discernment, able to following pastoral and team leadership, and have the "time" to spend in preparation for ministry to others.

6. Deliverance Team members must know their gifts and calling and the strengths the team members bring. They must be sensitive to the leading and guidance of the Holy Spirit. It is best to have a team leader, though that can change from time to time.

7. Deliverance Team members must be true worshippers yet able to pay attention to details in the worship service. They must sharpen their spiritual sensitivity.

8. Because deliverance ministry is hard work, team members should be allowed to take "a leave" from it to refresh and rest for periods of time.

9. Deliverance Team members should be male and female, and learn to work in teams of two.

10. Team members must be a member of a local church for proper spiritual covering and in right relationship with pastoral leadership.

11. Team members must be physically clean and not offensive to those they minister to. (breath and body)

12. Team members must not be judgmental for nothing surprises them! (SHOCK PROOF) They learn that demons are great actors and love attention.

13. Team should be prepared with throw cloths to cover persons, Kleenex, small bags or buckets if persons throw up, cups of water to drink if needed, anointing oil and even a room to take persons to if further deliverance is needed. No task is too small.

14. A medical person on the deliverance team is always a plus especially if they are able to determine what is a spiritual vs. physical manifestation.

15. It is a good practice to have communion before Deliverance crusades and events where demons are going to be confronted. Communion is powerful tool that brings the tangible presence of Jesus many times in the services.

16. Deal with team defectors and betrayal among the team immediately. It always hurts, but do not let discord and dissension take root. Never sacrifice the ministry or whole team for one or two people.

17. There are no super stars on the ministry team. Jesus Christ is the only Star. Guard against pride because you have had some victories. Remember we are not the Christ. Do not touch the gold or the glory for yourself. Freely you received and so you also freely give. Do not merchandize the ministry. Protect the team and recognize the "Simon spirit."

Beginning Definitions

Familiar Terms We will be Using in Deliverance

Deliverance - (I John 3:8) Deliverance is the method, or process ordained by God, by which Jesus gave the Church power to destroy the works of the devil and to set the captives free. Deliverance is the "casting out of devils/demons/unclean spirits" from human beings.

Usually demons have gained a level of influence or control over the person's body, by entering (by legal right of some kind) into the victims body or their "house." (Matthew 12:43-44)

Furthermore, where there is deliverance, it is a sign that "the kingdom of God has come upon you." Jesus put emphasis on the ministry of deliverance before He ascended back to heave in Mark 16:17, and gave all believers the authority over demons, and made it clear that "those who believe in His Name, will drive out demons."

DEMONS - Demons are referred to as "unclean spirits" in the King James Bible many times. They are fallen angels, as well as disembodied spirits that roam the earth looking for human beings as well as animals to inhabit.

They seek to control individuals (Ephesians 2:1-2), governments or political arenas (Daniel 10:13,20), and world events (John 12:31 and Ephesians 6:11-12, Colossians 2:8). Their mission is to "kill, steal and destroy" the human race. (John 10:10) Demons affect non Christians (Eph. 2:2) and Christians (Ephesians 6:11-12) Demons cannot possess (own) the spirit of a Christian, but we are body, soul and spirit and can be afflicted in other areas.

Demons can torment the mind, the will, the emotions and the body of believers if we give them legal ground or access into our lives. The Bible is clear that demons can enter into believers: Read Luke 13:10-17; Acts 5:3, I Corinthians 5:5, I Corinthians 10:20, II Corinthians 11:3,4, I Timothy 4:1, Galatians 3:1 and II Peter 2:1-22. Just because a Christian has demons operating in their lives does not mean they are not saved.

It means that they will not be able to reach their full potential in Christ with so much demonic control and influence. It means there are rooms in their "house" that unclean activity is still going on.

DEMONIZATION- The affliction and unclean activity in a Christian is called demonization not possession. It is illegal entry of unclean spirits that control and influence them more than the Holy Spirit's control and infilling. Demonization can occur when Christians are not filled with the Holy Spirit. The church is full of demonized believers, even pastors and church leaders. Read Luke 13:10-17, the story of the bent over woman for 18 years going to church. We will study further the signs of demonization in believers. Ephesians 6:10-17 is key for believers keeping on the whole armor of God.

I believe this keeps believers from being demonized. We also read in the Old Testament the life of King Saul in I Samuel 16:15 and the account of his demonization, troubled by an evil spirit. This is one of the earlier cases in scripture of a believer or man of God being demonized.

SPIRITUAL WARFARE - An advanced and **mature level of prayer** and intercession that removes demonic strongholds that are blinding individuals, false religions, cities and nations from receiving the gospel of Jesus Christ. (Read II Corinthians 4:4-5)

MANIFEST- A term that means the demons are acting out or display or demonstrate their presence in a person or a place. A manifestation is the symptom or evidence that there is a demonic presence.

How to Determine if you are Under Spiritual Attack

1. Your intercession and prayer life becoming ineffective and you are really struggling to pray and concentrate on spiritual things.

2. Your church attendance and worship is interrupted by minor things

3. Your are missing corporate or group prayer more and more

4. Bible Study and Worship becomes inconsistent and more sporadic

5. Loss of interest in spiritual things that were once very important to you; excuses.

6. Lack of conviction and lack of repentance

7. Detachment and absentee spirits set in

8. No accountability for your actions

9. No longer open to the counsel and wisdom of those over you; dull of hearing.

10. Lacking and loss of interest in fellowship

11. Convenience is more important than commitment to Christ and vision

12. Sudden loss of desire for spiritual things that were meeting your needs

13. Going back to the "vomit" of what you once left and could not tolerate

14. Lack of walking in truth and transparency with leadership and other saints especially the deliverance team

15. You begin to turn against deliverance ministry and disdain it as not necessary

16. Loss of spiritual vision and vitality

17. You are becoming evasive and invisible in the ministry

18. You feel it no longer takes "all that" to do deliverance or walk in holiness

19. You have come under attack physically and mentally

20. Feeling isolated more and more and like you are not part of the group

DISCUSSION QUESTIONS

1. In what ways can a deliverance team member compromise with the enemy and sleep with the enemy which in turn compromises the ministry team?

2. What is the danger of having been involved in a heavy deliverance ministry and then leaving the ministry to back to lesser accountability and compromise?

3. How do you respond to people who don't understand your calling to deliverance ministry?

4. How has the ministry of healing and deliverance changed your life personally?

5. Do you feel you have the "brave heart" anointing? What persons in the Bible flowed in that anointing and what motivated them all?

11. Another reason deliverance is a process and not an instant event, is because the Lord wants to prove what is really in our hearts. This is true of the deliverance worker and the one receiving prayer.

12. I have seen some people come for deliverance and if it does not happen in one session they go away, and never return. Pride and rebellion are major hindrances to becoming free from evil spirits. Through deliverance God will force the spirits to surface. Until repentance and humility emerge, we will continue to be vexed by these spirits.

13. Disobedience, stubbornness, pride and rebellion will hinder your deliverance.

14. We must develop a complete hatred for demons that at any price we will submit completely to the Word of God. One cannot have a tolerant attitude towards demons, idolatry, perversions and other sins.

15. Another reason deliverance takes so long is that some evil spirits are stronger and more difficult to conquer than others.

16. Another reason is found in Exodus when God said He would drive their enemies out little by little. The Lord desires spiritual growth before further deliverance can be received in an area. God is not just concerned with how much

deliverance you can receive, but also how much you can possess and maintain. God's people are to drive out the enemy and possess the land. Exodus 23:26-28.

17. It is critical to be led by the Holy Spirit in doing all deliverances.

18. Remember first deliverance, then holy living according to the Word of God; then we begin to possess our possessions.

19. Another reason deliverance takes so long is that God wants us to spend time patiently ministering to one another. Deliverance forces believers to spend time ministering to one another.

20. You must love, embrace and get on the floor if necessary to free others. This is what is sorely needed as we minister to one another.

_____

_____

_____

_____

_____

_____

_____

_____

_____

_____

_____

_____

_____

_____

1. (True/False) The law of double reference is the principle of associating unrelated ideas that are separated by long periods of time? _____

2. (True/False) According to Job 38:7 the "Sons of God" are fallen angels? _____

3. Who cast the Fallen Angels according to Revelation 12:4 to the Earth?   (x the correct answer) ___God ____Satan ___ The Dragon

4. According to Luke 10:1, which word is not a defined translation for "City" ___The Third Heaven ___ A town with Walls ___ Warfare

5. _____ of the angels that rebelled took on ranks, forms and positions throughout the Universe. (Fill in the blank)

6. In the rank of angels, how many Spheres must be examined? _____

7. Which is not a division of satanic forces according to Ephesians 6:12? ___Powers ___Demons ___World (rulers) ___Wicked Spirits

8. What forces are being directed in the Church of Jesus Christ? _____

9. In what sphere do the 7 archangels reside ? _____

10. What angels are said to have the ability to inspire us to art or science?
_____

11. (True/False) The Ante-Chaotic Age can be traced back to specific dates and times throughout the Bible?_____

12. What man is responsible for the "Gap Theory" _____

13. Whom did God first give dominion over the Earth to? ___Adam ___ Mankind ___Angels ___The Devil

14. Can Angels die? _____ (Yes/No)
15. When did Satan fall? ___ Before Adam and Eve ___After Adam and Eve ___ Before the World was Formed

16. How many times is the word Tartarus found in the Bible? _____

17. Where is the final destination place for fallen angels in Tartarus?
_____

18. Until the death and resurrection of Jesus, where are the righteous dead kept?
_____

19. Name the Greek and Hebrew term for hell _____ (Greek)
_____ (Hebrew)

20. What is known as the bottomless pit?
___The Abyss ___Gehenna ___Hell ___ Purgatory

21. Why did Satan attack the children of Adam and Eve?
_____

22. How does Satan seduce an appeal to man's spiritual desires?
_____

23. According to Genesis 3:10 and 11 what began to rule Man? _____

24. What scripture text shows how a Believer can be deceived into dual leadings ?
_____

25. (True/False) In testing the spirits all truth is in harmony with all teachings in the world?_____

26. (True/False) Sin can represent a person place or thing? _____

27. (True/False) Demons were not directly involved in the murder of Cain? _____

28. (True/False) Words like "possessed" could cause confusion to Believers and non-believers? _____

29. What does it mean to defile? _____

30. What causes spiritual infections?
_____

31. (True/False) Thinking it's all demons is a unbalanced way of thinking. _____

32. (True/False) A Deliverance team must first go through on going Deliverance themselves.
_____

33. What destroys a Deliverance Ministry? _____

34. Match

_____ Deliverance   _____Spiritual Warfare
_____ Demons   _____ Manifest
_____Demonization

A- in advance and mature level of prayer and intercession that removes demonic strongholds
B- the method or process ordained by God Church power to destroy the works of the devil and to set the captives free
C- the affliction and unclean activity in a Christian
D- unclean spirits
E- the acting out or display demonstration of a demonic presence in a person or place

35. Which is a effect of being under a spiritual attack? (x) all that apply

___ Loss of Vision (spiritually)   ___Sudden lost of desire for spiritual things ___ No accountability
_____ All of the above

36. What is the purpose of the anointing that is upon us?
_____
_____

37. According to Ephesians 6:14-18 what are our defensive weapons of our warfare ?
_____
_____

38. What reveals source of an attack?_____

39. (True/False)The Discerning of spirits is used to just deserve an angel or spiritual beings?
_____

40.It takes effort on our behalf to function in the gift of faith? (yes/no)_____
41. How is the spirit of infirmity often exposed?
_____

42.Is deliverance the manifestation of the Gift of Working of Miracles? (yes/no) _____

43. What steps should you take when you are given a prophecy concerning something you know nothing about?

_____
_____

44. What is the only way the enemy can attack a believer and cause them to need deliverance in a balanced deliverance perspective?

_____

45. (True/False) Prophetic words that supersedes the authority of a husband/wife is a prophetic danger that could damage? _____

46. What is a spirit guide?

_____

47. How can a pastor transfer spirits to his congregation?

_____

48. Define Territorial Spirit:

_____
_____

49. The powers gained from the assistance of evil spirits is defined as

_____.

50. In Acts 8 who caused the sickness throughout Samaria?
___Saten ___Simon ___Territorial Spirit

Answer Key

1. F
2. T
3. The Dragon
4. The Third Heaven
5. ⅓
6. Two
7. Demons
8. Wicked Spirits
9. 2nd
10. Principalities
11. F
12. Thomas Chalmers
13. angels
14. No
15. After Adam and Eve
16. 1
17. Lake of Fire
18. Abraham's Bosom
19. Hades or Sheol
20. The Abyss
21. He did not know who the Redeemer was
22. Disguising himself as an angel of Light
23. The mind
24. Matthew 16:13-17, 21- 23
25. F
26. T
27. F
28. T
29. Make Unclean
30. When you give the enemy rights to your body or soul
31. T
32. T
33. Contamination
34. B, D, C, A, E (Beginning top left)
35. All of Them
36. Destroy the works of the devil

37. Girdle of Truth, the breastplate of righteousness, the shoes of peace and the helmet of salvation
38. Word of knowledge
39. F
40. No
41. The ability to keep running in a family
42. Yes
43. Take caution, do not let it get you upset, ask God to reveal it to you
44. Through misuse or misunderstanding how the gifts operate
45. T
46. A spirit that communicates with the Dead
47. When the pastor does not resist the enemy
48. Spirit influence regions, places or environments
49. Sorcery
50. Territorial spirits

Written By: Apostle Ivory L. Hopkins

P.O. Box 81

Harbeson, Delaware 19951

Evelyn Hopkins Contact: 302-542-2047

evelynhopkins@comcast.net or ivoryhopkins@comcast.net

www.pilgrimsministry.org

Made in the USA
Columbia, SC
18 November 2024

46889534R00030